36 STRANGE LITTLE ANIMALS WAITING TO EAT

WITH SIMPLE LITTLE RECIPES TO MAKE

**Thanks to Frances Cleary for advice and help with the recipes,
and to the two young testers, Felicity and Clemency Jacques.**
Roz Denny

Text copyright © 1992 Roz Denny
Illustrations copyright © 1992 Graham Percy

Book design by Lisa Tai
Cover design by Lynn Pieroni
Edited by Ann ffolliott

Published in 1992 by
Stewart, Tabori & Chang, Inc.
575 Broadway, New York, New York 10012

Library of Congress Cataloging-in-Publication Data
Percy, Graham.
36 strange little animals waiting to eat, with simple little
recipes to make / conceived and illustrated by Graham Percy:
recipes by Roz Denny.
p. cm.
Summary: Unusual animals such as the Honey-Toed Sprowt and
the Plum-Tummied Chump provide recipes for their favorite dishes.

ISBN 1-55670-272-8

1. Cookery–Juvenile literature. [1. Cookery] I. Denny, Roz.
II. Title. III. Title: Thirty-six strange little animals waiting to
eat, with simple little recipes to make.
TX652.5.P397   1992
841.5'123–dc20   92-358
                                       CIP
                                       AC

Distributed in the U.S. by Workman Publishing,
708 Broadway, New York, New York 10003
Distributed in Canada by Canadian Manda Group,
P.O. Box 920 Station U, Toronto, Ontario M8Z 5P9

Printed in Singapore

10 9 8 7 6 5 4 3 2 1

36 STRANGE LITTLE ANIMALS WAITING TO EAT

WITH SIMPLE LITTLE RECIPES TO MAKE

CONCEIVED AND ILLUSTRATED BY GRAHAM PERCY
RECIPES BY ROZ DENNY

STEWART, TABORI & CHANG
NEW YORK

Six sensible little hints from thirty-six strange little animals

1   Read the recipes through first and get together all the ingredients, utensils, pans, and baking sheets you will need. Wash your hands before handling food.

2   Measure carefully. Level cups of flour and sugar after filling. Get all the peeling and chopping done before you start cooking.

3   Make sure an adult is in the kitchen with you to see that everything is okay, especially if you are using sharp knives, mixers, food processors, or the oven or stove.

4   When using sharp knives, make sure your fingers aren't in the way.

5   Remember – stoves, ovens, pans, and steam can burn, so make sure your hands (or paws) are well wrapped or covered when you touch or pick up hot things.

6   Wash up your dirty pots and pans, and clear away neatly after eating.

Most of all – have fun and enjoy your food, just like these strange little animals do!

Hot bagel with honey-raisin cream cheese

The Honey-Toed Sprowt is drooling at the thought of his favorite breakfast. He likes to carry bagels home from the store on his nose. That way he can breathe in the delicious smell and imagine every mouthful of his first-choice meal. He eats these every day. Rain or shine, whatever the weather, they just taste so good.

When he's home, he gets together:

- I plain bagel (except on Sundays when he has a poppy seed one)
- 2 tablespoons of cream cheese, at room temperature
- 2 teaspoons of honey
- I tablespoon of raisins
- a tiny paw pinch of ground cinnamon

And now *it's* time to start pr*e*paring *it*:

1. First, he puts the bagel on a cutting board and cuts it in half lengthwise. He does this very carefully because knives are sharp and can cut his padded paws.

2. He puts the cream cheese in a bowl and stirs it with a spoon until it is nice and soft.

3. He spoons the honey onto the cheese, making sure it doesn't run down his front toes. He sprinkles in the raisins and mixes everything well.

4. Then he pops the two bagel halves onto the toaster and toasts them until they are a nice golden brown.

5. He takes out the toasted bagels (carefully, because they are quite hot), lays them on his plate, and spreads the honey-raisin cream cheese on top.

6. Now, all he has to do is sprinkle a little cinnamon on both halves and eat them quickly, before the cream cheese melts too much.

Pancakes with apple sauce and ice cream

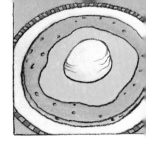

The Pancake-Eared Inkstump is waiting for Mother to cook his favorite dessert. Mother Inkstump likes cooking pancakes because all the ingredients are in her cupboard or refrigerator and she has plenty of ice cream in her freezer. Inkstump Junior likes to watch the runny batter change into little, light pancakes.

He helps her get ready:

I cup of all-purpose flour

I teaspoon of baking powder

I tablespoon of sugar

I egg

¾ cup of milk

a little vegetable oil, for frying

a jar of apple sauce, to serve on top of the pancakes

scoops of ice cream (because he's been very helpful at home)

Mother Inkstump makes the pancakes by:

1. Sifting the flour into a large mixing bowl and letting her son sprinkle the sugar over it. Then he makes a well in the flour in the middle of the bowl.

2. Junior cracks the egg into a cup, makes sure it is okay, puts the egg in the well in the flour, and pours in half the milk.

3. Using a whisk, Junior mixes the flour, egg, and half the milk together, then continues mixing, adding more milk until it is all used up and the mixture is smooth.

4. Mother Inkstump slowly heats a heavy frying pan on the stove and brushes a little oil over it. She carefully pours two tablespoons of batter at a time onto the hot pan.

5. When the batter is no longer runny and holes appear all over the top, Inkstump Junior flips over the pancakes, using a slotted spatula, and cooks the other side.

6. Mother Inkstump and Junior cook the rest of the batter, and they eat the pancakes, three or four at a time, with apple sauce and ice cream.

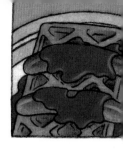

Waffles with sausages and best blueberry jelly

The Old Smooth-Nosed Grumpit is very particular.
Every Saturday morning he has to have waffles and sausages.
He says only Mrs. Grumpit knows just how he likes his sausages,
which should be a nice mid-brown and not too burnt.

In the kitchen, Mrs. Grumpit gathers:

2 breakfast sausages

1 large frozen waffle

a little butter

2 teaspoons of good and fruity blueberry jelly

Then Mrs. Grumpit starts to cook:

1   First, she heats the broiler. Then she lays the sausages on the rack and puts them under the heat. She holds the pan with a thick mitt so her dainty, furry paws won't burn.

2   She broils the sausages under medium heat for about five minutes. Then she removes the pan and turns the sausages with a spoon and fork, and returns the pan to the broiler.

3   After another five minutes, she removes the pan with a thick mitt. She uses the spoon and fork to put the sausages on a paper towel.

4   Now, Mrs. Grumpit puts the waffle in a toaster. She pushes it down and up it pops two minutes later – all crunchy and golden brown.

5   She places the waffle on a plate, spreads a little butter on it, arranges the two sausages on top, and spoons the jelly over them.

6   The Old Smooth-Nosed Grumpit eats the waffle with a knife and fork, then wipes any jelly off his whiskers with his crisp, white napkin.

Hot oatmeal with raisins or chocolate chips

The Shaggy-Topped Slumpstumps find it hard to get up in the early morning. They just can't seem to shake themselves awake – until Mother Slumpstump sets down two steaming bowls of hot oatmeal at the table. Father Slumpstump likes to add yogurt and raisins to his, while Junior sleepily stirs in a few chocolate chips.

To make the oatmeal, Mother Slumpstump gets out:

I cup of quick-cooking oatmeal

I cup of milk

I cup of water

2 teaspoons of sugar or honey

For Father Slumpstump, she gets:

I tablespoon of plain yogurt

I tablespoon of raisins

a pinch of ground nutmeg

For Slumpstump Junior, she gets:

I tablespoon of chocolate chips

a pinch of ground cinnamon

Mother Slumpstump makes the oatmeal like this:

1 She puts the oatmeal into a medium-sized saucepan and stirs in the milk and water. She brings the mixture slowly to a boil on the stove, carefully stirring it every so often so it does not get lumpy.

2 When the oatmeal is nice and thick, and starts to bubble, she turns the heat down and cooks it for two minutes. She stirs in the sugar, although sometimes she uses honey.

3 Using a thick oven mitt, she carries the saucepan to the table where she has already laid out two bowls and spoons. Eagerly Mr. Slumpstump watches as his bigger portion is poured into his bowl.

4 Junior still has his eyes closed while his oatmeal is poured into his bowl, and it is not until Mother sprinkles chocolate chips and cinnamon into it that he slowly lifts his head and starts to stir everything together.

5 Father Slumpstump stirs in the yogurt, raisins, and nutmeg – and in no time at all, both Slumpstumps are eating their creamy breakfasts.

Starry beans on rye toast

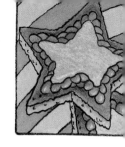

The Sweet-Nosed Billybunk says "Eating well is cool" as she heads for home to prepare herself a light meal. Today she wants baked beans with cheese, but her meal must have *style*, like her star-studded jacket. So, she cuts the rye bread and cheese slice into star shapes.

Then she starts to cook:

First, Ms. Billybunk gets:

2 slices of rye bread

1 slice of Swiss cheese

a little cheese spread

½ cup of baked beans

2 star-shaped cookie cutters, one large and one small

1 Using the larger cookie cutter, she cuts out two stars from the rye bread and throws away the outside of the bread and crusts.

2 Using the small cutter, she cuts out two stars from the cheese slice and puts them to one side. She doesn't want to waste the rest of the cheese slice, so she chops it up quite finely to use later.

3 She toasts the rye stars under a hot broiler, because the fine points of the star might stick in a toaster. When they are light brown on both sides, she carefully removes them and spreads them with a little cheese spread and sprinkles the chopped up Swiss cheese over them.

4 Meanwhile, Ms. Billybunk heats the beans in a small saucepan on the stove until they are quite hot, then she spoons the beans onto the toast stars.

5 She tops each warm bean star with a cheese star, which melts a little on the hot beans. Mmmm – it does look so good.

Fried egg-in-a-nest

The Green-Eyed Quilch just loves to read. He has little time to cook and eat. Besides, he likes his food neat and orderly, and cooking can be very messy. So he often frys an egg in the middle of a slice of bread, so it doesn't spread all over the pan.

For this, all he needs is:

1 small fresh egg

salt and pepper

1 thick slice of bread

a little vegetable oil

a pat of butter

a pinch of dried dill weed or a little fresh chopped parsley, when he feels like it

When he's feeling hungry, this is how he cooks it:

1 First, the Quilch cracks the egg into a cup and sprinkles a little salt and pepper on it, but doesn't mix it.

2 Then, using a large round cookie cutter, he presses down in the middle of the bread and takes out the center, which he puts aside to nibble later.

3 He pours about a tablespoon of oil into a small skillet and very carefully heats it up, then puts in the bread slice with the hole.

4 As the bread starts to fry, the Quilch turns the heat down and slowly pours the egg into the hole, making sure none spills out. Then he covers the skillet with a lid and cooks the egg and bread for about two minutes.

5 He carefully removes the lid, making sure the steam doesn't burn his hand, and, using a slotted spatula, loosens the fried bread and egg and lifts it onto a plate.

6 For a finishing touch, he tops the egg with a small pat of butter which melts, and sprinkles on a pinch of dill or parsley. Then he props up a book on the table in front of him to read while he eats his egg-in-a-nest with a knife and fork.

Croissant with ham and Swiss cheese

The Beautiful Three-Eared Munch loves hot chocolate, conversation, and crisp croissants from her favorite café. There she sits delicately munching her mid-morning snack while she chats with her closest friend, the Elegant Gold-Scaled Honk.

She watches the café owner assemble:

a large, fresh croissant

2 thin slices of Swiss cheese

2 wafer-thin slices of smoked ham

Making her croissant sandwich is quite easy:

1. The café owner carefully slices the delicious and buttery croissant in half lengthwise with a knife and opens it up.

2. He checks that his oven is on low and is nice and warm. He lays the croissant out on a flat baking sheet.

3. First, he puts the cheese slices on one half and the ham on top of that. Then he puts on the croissant top, and pops it into the oven for a few minutes, until the cheese melts.

4. The beautiful Three-Eared Munch watches intently while the café owner pulls out the baking sheet, using a thick oven mitt so his hands don't burn. He puts the wonderful cheesy croissant on a plate and cuts it in half.

5. He pours his favorite customer a steaming cup of hot chocolate and rushes out to her table with her order. The conversation stops – it is time for chocolate and a croissant. Miss Munch thought it all looked so easy that maybe she will make her own cheese and ham croissant tomorrow.

12

Two cheese dips with veggie sticks

The Two Purple-Furred Frizzles usually offer their guests a choice of two cheese dips with perfectly cut thin vegetable sticks. Mr. and Mrs. Frizzle love color in their food, so they choose pretty red, green, and orange vegetables, which they arrange in a circle around the two bowls of dip.

The ingredients are simple:

1 8-ounce package of cream cheese, at room temperature

2 tablespoons of light cream or plain yogurt

¼ cup of grated Cheddar cheese

¼ cup of grated Swiss cheese

1 red bell pepper

2 medium-sized carrots

¼ of a fresh cucumber

An hour or two before guests are due:

1 They put the cream cheese and cream or yogurt into a bowl and mix the two together with a fork until very smooth. They spoon half this mixture into another bowl and mix it with the Cheddar cheese.

2 In the first bowl they mix the Swiss cheese into the remaining mixture, then they spoon both dips into small, pretty glass bowls and set these on a large flat plate.

3 Mr. and Mrs. Frizzle take turns preparing the vegetables. They each peel a carrot, slice off the top, then cut it into long, thin sticks.

4 Mrs. Frizzle carefully cuts the bell pepper in half, pulls out the seeds and stalks (which she throws away), and cuts the pepper into thin strips, about the same size as the carrot sticks.

5 Mr. Frizzle cuts the cucumber in half lengthwise, then cuts each piece in half again, so he has four long pieces. He carefully cuts the seeds out, then slices each long pieces into sticks.

6 The Frizzles arrange the pretty colored sticks around the bowls of dip, place them on the table, and relax quietly until their guests arrive.

Slippy green soup

Mrs. Grizzle and her Little Velvet Grizzles are excited. "Dad's cooking supper! And, it's our favorite, green pea soup, to which we can add our own secret ingredients!" Mr. Grizzle's is shredded spinach, because it looks so pretty floating in the soup. The little Grizzles have their own ideas, but they all enjoy eating the soup with saltines, which they break into the soup so the pieces look like little fish.

Mr. Grizzle's ingredients are:

1 (11-ounce) can of condensed green pea soup

milk to fill the empty soup can

about 1 ounce of fresh green spinach

8 saltine crackers

The little Grizzles, Guy and Gertie, like:

2 tablespoons of canned or frozen corn and pimiento

2 tablespoons of chopped ham

Mr. Grizzle makes the family's soup like this:

1. He opens the can and spoons the thick soup into a medium-sized saucepan. He fills the empty can with milk, which he gradually mixes in with a wooden spoon while he heats the pan up slowly.

2. Then he fills the can with water halfway and stirs that into the soup as well.

3. Although the spinach leaves look clean, Mr. Grizzle asks little Guy to wash them well in a colander under cold running water. Guy turns them with his hands and picks off any thick stalks.

4. Mr. Grizzle shakes the leaves and gathers them together in a bunch, which he then places on a chopping board and shreds finely with a sharp knife.

5. He brings the soup to a gentle boil, adds the spinach shreds, and simmers it all for only a minute, until the shreds just wilt.

6. Mr. Grizzle pours the soup into four warmed bowls. The children add their special ingredients. Guy Grizzle adds corn and pimiento to his and Gertie stirs the ham into hers. Mrs. Grizzle joins them and they all eat the soup with crackers.

14

Spaghetti with hot dogs and Cheddar cheese

The Cheeky-Faced Lumpsring is in a mischievous mood. Who can he tease today? Maybe Old Mr. Grumpit as he sets out to buy his particular best blueberry jelly. But first, he cooks himself a nice, quick, sustaining snack – nothing too difficult, because he must get out soon.

He looks in his cupboard *and* refrigerator *and* pulls out:

1 small (8-ounce) can of spaghetti with tomato sauce

1 hot dog

a small jar of mild yellow mustard (he's feeling devilish)

a jar of dried thyme

a chunk of Cheddar cheese

QUICK – he's only got 10 minutes:

1   Using a can opener, he opens the can with a steady hand so none of the contents spill out, then he removes the lid carefully. Opened cans can be so sharp. He pours the spaghetti into a small saucepan and heats it up slowly on the stove.

2   He puts the cheese on a board and, with a knife, cuts enough small cubes to fill a third of a cup. Then he wraps the rest of the cheese in plastic wrap and puts it back in the refrigerator.

3   With a wooden spoon, he gives the spaghetti a stir. Then he puts the hot dog on the board and cuts it into small pieces with the knife.

4   He adds the hot dog pieces to the spaghetti and spoons in a small teaspoon of the mustard, then sprinkles in just a pinch of the thyme and stirs it all together while it heats up.

5   When the spaghetti mixture has bubbled gently for about a minute, he removes the pan from the heat (carefully) and adds the cheese, stirring it a little – not too much because he likes his cheese in nice, soft chunks.

6   He pours it all into a bowl and eats it right away. He must get to the corner store before Mr. Grumpit arrives.

Big herby burgers

The Plum-Tummied Chump is always hungry. There is nothing he likes better than chomping his way through a big, juicy, homemade burger, which he makes extra tasty with herbs and soy sauce. He likes to make three at a time, so he has two to spare — either for friends who drop by or to freeze for other meals.

For three BIG herby burgers he needs:

½ pound of ground beef

1 tablespoon of soy sauce

1 teaspoon of dried oregano or marjoram

a little oil, for cooking

for each burger, he also has—

1 seeded hamburger bun, split in half

1 small tomato

1 small lettuce leaf

1 teaspoon of mayonnaise

Making Big Herby Burgers *is* simple:

1 The Chump puts the ground beef in a bowl and adds the soy sauce and herbs. He mixes the ingredients together with his clean, washed hooves.

2 He divides the meat into three balls all about the same size. Then he squashes them flat into round patties, as neat and round as he can.

3 The Chump wraps two of the burgers separately in plastic wrap and puts them in the freezer.

4 He heats the skillet up carefully with just a small amount of oil, puts the remaining burger on a slotted spatula, and lowers it gently into the pan.

5 He cooks the burger over medium heat for two minutes on one side, then flips it over with the spatula and cooks it for one minute more. The Chump removes the burger and puts it on a paper towel.

6 Meanwhile, he lightly toasts the burger bun and asks his Mom to cut the tomato into slices. Then, he puts the lettuce leaf on the bottom half of the bun and spreads the mayonnaise on the top half. On top of the lettuce he slips the burger, arranges the tomato slices over that, and . . . wham! Slams the bun top onto the burger.

7 Great, now it's time to eat. Mom ties his napkin around his neck and he sinks his tusks deep down into the big herby burger.

Fish sticks with cucumber and carrot scales

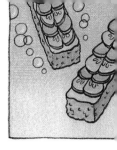

The Elegant Gold-Scaled Honk just loves to be seen, so all who meet her can admire the smooth, shiny scales she polishes each morning. This lunchtime two of her most elegant friends will be calling to nibble at a dainty light meal of fish sticks, spread with mayonnaise and topped with thin slices of fresh vegetables.

From the refrigerator and freezer she gathers:

1 small carrot

a small piece of cucumber

6 fish sticks

a bottle of vegetable oil

a jar of mayonnaise

3 cherry tomatoes

She prepares and cooks the dish just before her guests arrive:

1   She places the carrot and cucumber on a chopping board. Using a vegetable peeler, she scrapes the carrot clean, carefully chops off the top and tail, and cuts it into thin slices.

2   Then she cuts eight thin slices from the cucumber. She cuts the carrot and cucumber slices in half, then in half again to make quarters.

3   Now, she puts the fish sticks on the broiler pan, and using a pastry brush, brushes them with a little oil. Using an oven mitt, she puts the broiler pan under the heat.

4   She broils these for three minutes on one side, and using her oven mitt, she removes the broiler pan and turns the fish sticks over with a spoon and fork. She cooks them for another three minutes.

5   She puts the fish sticks back on the chopping board, spreads a little mayonnaise on top of each, and lays carrot and cucumber slices on top in alternate layers, neatly and quite close together.

6   She puts two fish sticks on each plate, then cuts the tomatoes into halves and lays these at each end.

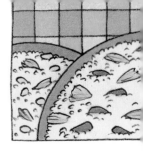

Tuna and rice salad

The Little Family of Whispering Winks speak in soft voices discussing their next delicious dinner because the walls of their house are so thin. Mrs. Wink doesn't feel like swimming to the store, so she makes a salad using ingredients she already has on hand. Her two sons, Will and Wayne, like to help Mom after she's cooked the rice.

From her cupboard Mrs. Wink takes:

1 cup of long grain rice

1 (7-ounce) can of tuna

1 teaspoon of salt

1 tablespoon of vinaigrette dressing

2 tablespoons of mayonnaise

1 tablespoon of sour cream

2 scallions

1 small carrot

Will and Wayne Wink want:

1 tablespoon of corn

1 tablespoon of cooked green beans

Mrs. Wink cooks it like this:

1 She combines the rice and salt with two cups of cold water in a medium-sized saucepan and puts it on the stove to boil. When it starts to bubble, she stirs it carefully, then covers it and turns the heat down to low.

2 After fifteen minutes, she turns the heat off and leaves the rice for five minutes, still covered. Then she removes the lid, carefully so the steam doesn't burn her, and stirs in the vinaigrette, then lets the rice cool.

3 Meanwhile, Mrs. Wink opens the can of tuna, drains off the liquid, then pours it into a large mixing bowl. Will flakes it up with a fork and Wayne mixes the mayonnaise and sour cream together.

4 Mrs. Wink peels and chops the scallions finely and peels the carrot. Both boys want to grate it, so they take turns, using the coarse side of the grater.

5 Then they add the mayonnaise, scallions, and grated carrot to the tuna and mix it all together. Mrs. Wink adds the rice and they all take turns stirring it up.

6 Mrs. Wink divides the salad among three plates. She wants hers plain. The boys sprinkle the corn and beans on top of their delicious salads.

English muffin pizzas

The Quivering Sugareenoes

are very excited because it's Saturday and that's the day Grandma comes over and cooks their favorite lunch – English muffin pizzas. She always lets her grandchildren choose their own toppings.

The three small Sugareenoes get together:

6 ounces of mozzarella cheese

4 English muffins

½ cup of spaghetti sauce

For toppings they each choose from:

2 slices of Canadian bacon

I tablespoon of canned or frozen corn

I tablespoon of chopped cooked shrimp

I tablespoon of chopped cooked zucchini

8 small pepperoni slices

2 teaspoons of chopped scallion

Then Grandma Sugareenoe starts the cooking:

1 She cuts the cheese into slices as thin as she can and splits the muffins in half.

2 Meanwhile, the small Sugareenoes get their special toppings ready. The bacon needs frying in a small skillet – carefully, in case it spits. Then it's drained on paper towels and snipped into pieces with scissors.

3 The other toppings don't need much preparation apart from some chopping, so the Sugareenoes put them on small saucers, ready to top the hot muffins.

4 Grandma then lays the muffins out on a broiler pan and toasts them under a hot broiler, turning them once, until they are golden brown on both sides.

5 The small Sugareenoes spread Grandma's spaghetti sauce on the muffins, two teaspoons on each muffin, then top them with the cheese slices. Grandma likes hers plain.

6 The toppings are – bacon and corn on two, shrimp and zucchini on two, and pepperoni and scallion on two.

7 Grandma puts all the muffins back under the broiler until the cheese just melts. Quickly, she takes them from the pan with an oven mitt. The small Sugareenoes are all quivering with excitement at the thought of eating hot, fresh pizzas.

20

Crunchy macaroni and cheese

The Crumpled Kreepits think mealtime is the best time of the day because they all love to cook and eat together. One of their favorite family dishes is Macaroni and Cheese. Mother Kreepit likes it plain and simple, but the little Kreepits love being able to add special ingredients.

These are the ingredients the Kreepits need:

2 cups of uncooked macaroni

salt, for cooking

1 (11-ounce) can of condensed Cheddar cheese or tomato soup

milk to fill the empty soup can

1 cup of grated Cheddar cheese

3 tablespoons of crunchy croutons

Chris Kreepit adds:

2 tablespoons of flaked canned tuna

1 tablespoon of cooked peas

While Kirsty Kreepit adds:

1 small pepperoni sausage

1 small tomato

Then all together they cook:

1. They put a large saucepan of water on to boil, then add a teaspoon of salt. When the water boils, they pour in the macaroni, give it a good stir with a long wooden spoon, and return the water to a medium boil.

2. Chris Kreepit sets the kitchen timer for ten minutes. When the timer rings, the macaroni is cooked and his mother drains it in a colander.

3. Mother Kreepit puts the macaroni back into the pan and adds the soup. She fills the empty soup can with milk and stirs that into the macaroni mixture until it is nice and smooth.

4. She brings the whole lot back to a gentle simmer for two minutes, takes the pan off the stove, then asks Kirsty Kreepit to stir in the grated cheese until it has melted.

5. Mrs. Kreepit divides the macaroni equally among three bowls. She keeps her portion plain.

6. Chris stirs flaked tuna and peas into his, while Kirsty chops up the sausage and tomato and stirs those into hers. Then they all sprinkle the croutons over the macaroni and dig in quickly, before it gets cold.

Red jelly cushion cookies

The Crimson Cushiontop loves the smell of homemade cookies baking in the oven. He particularly loves the chewy red jelly center of these cookies, which he likes to nibble around and leave to the last delicious mouthful. With help from his big sister, the little Cushiontop loves to roll and cut out the dough. Sometimes he makes round ones and sometimes heart-shaped ones.

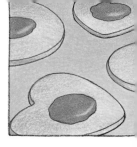

He measures out:

½ stick of butter, softened

½ cup of sugar

1 egg

1 teaspoon of vanilla extract

¾ cup of all-purpose flour

some soft, runny red jam,
either raspberry or strawberry

To mix and bake eight cookies:

1 The Cushiontop beats the butter, sugar, and vanilla in a mixer or food processor until light and creamy. Then he breaks the egg into a cup, beats it well with a fork, and pours half of it into the mixing bowl. He doesn't need the rest of the egg.

2 He scrapes the butter and sugar mixture into a bowl with a plastic spatula. Then he stirs in the flour to form a smooth dough, shapes it into a round ball, and chills it in the refrigerator for an hour or two, until it is firm.

3 When he is ready to cut out the cookies, the Cushiontop heats the oven to 375°F.

4 He sprinkles the counter with some flour. Using a rolling pin sprinkled with flour, the Cushiontop rolls out the dough until it is ½-inch thick. Every so often he loosens the dough with a long spatula and turns it to keep it nice and even, sprinkling the counter and rolling pin in between with more flour.

5 With a two-inch round or heart-shaped cookie cutter, the Cushiontop cuts out eight cookies. It's not possible to get them all out of one rolling, so he squashes the leftover dough into a smooth ball and rolls it out again.

6 He puts the cookies on a baking sheet and presses a hollow in the middle of each with his finger. Then he puts about half a teaspoon of the jelly in each hollow. He bakes the cookies for about fifteen minutes, until golden brown.

7 He takes the baking sheet from the oven, using an oven mitt, and lets them cool for a minute before removing them with a long metal spatula onto a cooling rack to crisp up.

Chicken salad pita sandwich

The Wandering Yumptee eats lots of sandwiches because wandering makes him so hungry. He especially likes to take a pita bread sandwich because he can slip it inside his pocket without the nice creamy filling spilling out. Sometimes, the Yumptee uses flaked tuna instead of chicken. Or, chopped hard-cooked egg and a few crushed corn chips to make it all nice and crunchy. He finds this sandwich very easy to eat with one paw.

While out walking he buys:

1 large white or whole wheat pita bread

1 small cooked chicken breast

Then from the refrigerator he gets:

2 lettuce leaves (which he washes well)

1 tablespoon of mayonnaise

2 teaspoons of ketchup

1 small dill pickle

1 small tomato, also washed well

Just before he wants to wander :

1   He cuts the pita bread in half and puts his paws inside each half to open the bread. He puts a lettuce leaf in each pita half.

2   On his chopping board, he removes the skin and bones from the chicken breast. Using a small sharp knife, he carefully cuts up the chicken meat into small pieces and saves half for tomorrow, wrapping it well in plastic wrap.

3   In a bowl he mixes the chicken up well with the mayonnaise and ketchup.

4   He puts the dill pickle on the board and cuts that in slices as thinly as he can. He cuts the tomato in thin slices too.

5   He spoons half the chicken mixture into one pita half, and half into the other. Then he puts the dill pickle and tomato on top of the chicken mixture and off he wanders.

Strawberry and banana yogurt soda

Th*e* Smiling Pintop's long elegant neck may be useful when it comes to looking over the heads of people, but her throat does get so dry! The solution, she thinks, is a long, cool iced yogurt soda sipped slowly through a thick straw.

It *takes* next to no time to get:

- 1 small, ripe banana
- 1 scoop of soft strawberry or vanilla ice cream
- 1 cup of strawberry-flavored yogurt drink
- a good handful of ice cubes
- a little lemon-lime soft drink, to fill the glass
- a sprig of fresh mint and a small fresh strawberry, to decorate, if the Pintop has them on hand

To mix *it all up is* easy:

1. The Pintop peels and slices the banana and pops it into a blender with the scoop of ice cream.

2. She switches on the machine for as long as it takes to count to 10, then turns off the machine and scrapes around the inside of the blender with a long-handled spoon.

3. She turns the blender on again, this time to the count of 5, and switches it off, then she puts in the yogurt drink and blends again to the count of 5.

4. She pulls out her tallest glass and drops in the handful of ice cubes from her freezer. Over this she puts the yogurt and banana mix.

5. Slowly she fills up the glass with the soft drink, then sticks in a thick, colorful straw and stirs everything around to mix it all together.

6. All that is needed to set it off splendidly is a sprig of fresh mint and a small strawberry, both of which she just happens to have in the refrigerator.

Juicy jello desserts

The Shy Little Long-Nosed Tribbles wish they could share two lovely recipes for gelatin desserts with you. One is Orange and Cranberry with Strawberries and the other is Cranberry and Orange with Blueberries. But the little Tribbles don't have the courage to tell you in person, so they have written the recipes down.

First, the Tribbles say you will need:

1 cup of orange juice

1 cup of cranberry juice

1 (3-ounce) package of orange-flavored gelatin

2 teaspoons of honey, if you want the dessert to be sweeter

8 medium-sized strawberries

1 cup of fresh blueberries

and 4 tall wine glasses
(Ask your mom if you can borrow them just for this. Mother Tribble says it's fine by her.)

And, this *is* how you should make the desserts:

1. Heat the orange juice and the cranberry juice separately, either in two saucepans on the stove, or in two separate bowls if you are using the microwave.

2. Divide the gelatin into two halves. When the juices are hot and steaming, sprinkle half of the gelatin into the orange juice and the rest into the cranberry.

3. Stir both until the gelatin has completely dissolved. If you like, add a teaspoon of honey to each and stir again. Let both gelatins cool for about an hour.

4. Cut the strawberries in half and set four halves aside. Put the rest into two wine glasses. Put six blueberries aside and put the rest into two more glasses.

5. Fill the glasses with the strawberries half way with the cranberry gelatin juice, and the blueberry glasses with the orange gelatin juice. Let the gelatin in the glasses set firmly in the refrigerator for about an hour.

6. Now, switch gelatins! Pour the rest of the cranberry gelatin juice on top of the orange and blueberry glasses, and the orange gelatin juice on top of the cranberry and strawberry, and return the glasses to the refrigerator. When they have set firmly, decorate with the strawberry halves and blueberries.

Crushed cookies in ice cream

The Two Little Soft-Faced Quincepigs like to create simple, easy desserts. Cyril Quincepig first thought of crushing up the last few chocolate cookies in the cookie jar and stirring them into his ice cream, then his wife Ellen added sliced pears and bananas. The secret is to add the cookies just before eating, so they stay nice and crunchy.

To make their easy dessert you will need:

3 scoops (about ½ pint) of soft vanilla ice cream

3 scoops (about ½ pint) of soft mint–chocolate chip ice cream

4 chocolate sandwich cookies, such as Oreos

1 small ripe pear

½ of a small ripe banana

on very special days
1 – 2 tablespoons of fresh raspberrries

It only takes a few minutes to put the desserts together:

1 The Quincepigs put vanilla ice cream in one mixing bowl and mint–chocolate chip in another.

2 They take two cookies each, and holding them over the bowls in their paws, break them into very small pieces. With large metal spoons, they stir the cookie crumbs into the two soft ice creams.

3 Ellen Quincepig carefully peels the pear and cuts it into quarters, slices out the cores, then chops the fruit into spoon-size mouthfuls.

4 Meanwhile, Cyril peels the half banana and slices it into thin rounds.

5 They scrape the ice cream into two dishes — vanilla for Cyril and mint–chocolate chip for Ellen. They scatter both pear pieces and banana rounds on each — and on special occasions put the raspberries on top. They eat the ice cream right away, before it melts.

27

Peanut butter cupcakes with cherry pink icing

The Little Purring Shutterblink

has the endearing quality of modesty, for she is a very fine cook but would never admit it – at least not in public. Her best recipe is for chocolate-flavored peanut butter cupcakes with pretty pink tops. She purrs with pleasure at the thought of making them so well because, in fact, they are quite easy to do and are very popular with her friends.

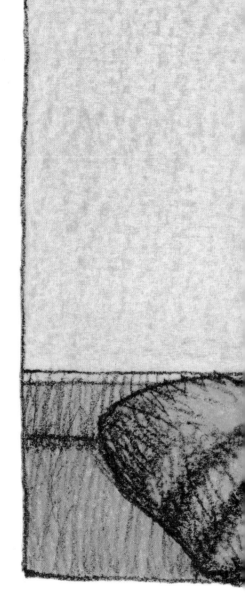

First, she measures out:

1 cup of all-purpose flour

2 tablespoons of cocoa powder

1½ teaspoons of baking powder

1 cup of sugar

½ cup of sunflower oil

2 eggs

1 teaspoon of vanilla extract

½ cup of milk

3 tablespoons of crunchy peanut butter

For the tops, she gets:

½ cup of confectioners' sugar

some warm water

a little red food coloring

6 candied cherries

It is quite simple to make her cupcakes:

1 Miss Shutterblink puts twelve paper baking cups into a muffin tin and turns the oven on to 375°F. She puts the flour, cocoa powder, and baking powder in a sifter and sifts the contents into a bowl.

2 With a large wooden spoon, she makes a well in the center of the flour mixture and sprinkles the sugar over it. Then she pours the oil into the middle of the well.

3 She cracks each egg on the side of the bowl, pulls the shells apart with her paws, and lets the eggs fall into the oil. She pours in the vanilla and milk, and spoons in the peanut butter.

4 The easy part is beating everything together until it is smooth and creamy. Miss Shutterblink gives it some extra beats, just to make quite sure.

5 Using two small spoons, she scoops the mixture into the paper baking cups until they are all about three-quarters full. Then with an oven mitt, she puts the tin into the oven for fifteen minutes.

6 Using oven mitts, she pulls the tin from the oven and presses the tops of the cakes. If they are springy, then she knows they are done; if not, she returns them to the oven for a few minutes more.

7 Miss Shutterblink removes the cupcakes to a cooling rack so they get quite cold while she makes the icing. She sifts the confectioners' sugar into a bowl, then pours a tablespoon of warm water and a single drop of food coloring into the sugar.

8 She mixes it all together, adding about another half-spoonful of water if it's a bit dry. The icing should be just runny but not too thick. Miss Shutterblink spoons icing on top of each cake. As a final touch, she cuts the cherries in half and puts one on top of each cake.

Vanilla pudding sea with rocks and icebergs

The Waddling Plumpkin likes thinking up new ways to serve food. He has all sorts of ideas and enjoys eating the results, which is why he is so fat. This time, he has thought of a way of making up a sea scene with his dessert and likes to watch it wobble as he waddles from the kitchen to the table. His recipe serves one plumpkin or four humans.

He uses:

1 3½-ounce package of vanilla pudding mix

3 cups of milk

¼ cup of raisins

24 miniature marshmallows

He puts his creation together like this:

1   He opens the pudding mix and shakes it into a medium-sized saucepan. Then he stirs in the milk, using a long-handled wooden spoon.

2   He puts the pan on the stove and slowly brings the contents to a boil while stirring carefully so he doesn't burn his hands. He likes to watch the mixture turn thick and creamy.

3   When it all starts to bubble, he removes the pan from the heat and continues to stir every so often, so a skin doesn't form. Then he covers the pan with plastic wrap and sets it on the counter until it cools off.

4   He removes the plastic wrap, stirs the pudding well to make it smooth again, and pours it into a large shallow bowl. He sets it in the refrigerator for an hour.

5   Finally, the Plumpkin positions the raisins as rocks on his sea of pudding and dots it with marshmallows to look like icebergs. As he waddles toward the table, he makes sure the bowl shakes.

Strawberries with hot chocolate dipping sauce

The Little Pink-Eyed Wingwing sits alone at the kitchen table, waiting for her special dessert to cool down. She's so hungry today that she doesn't want to share any of her ripe, juicy strawberries – which she dips, one by one, into her own secret-recipe chocolate sauce.

To make her treat, she gets together:

4 ounces of semisweet chocolate

¼ cup of light cream

1 tablespoon of honey

a few drops of vanilla extract

1 cup of ripe strawberries

Although *it's a secret,* she'd like you to know how the sauce is made:

1. She breaks the chocolate into pieces and puts them into a medium-sized heatproof glass bowl.

2. She pours the cream into the bowl and spoons in the honey. She only needs a few drops of vanilla extract, so she pours them gently and carefully into a teaspoon and then stirs this into the bowl.

3. Little Wingwing uses her microwave oven to melt the sauce. She puts the bowl, uncovered, into the oven and switches it onto full power for one minute.

4. She then removes the bowl carefully and stirs the contents with a spoon. It is still a bit lumpy so she puts the bowl back and cooks it again on full power for another minute.

5. Then she takes the bowl out, and stirs it again until it becomes a nice smooth and silky sauce. She pours it into a small, pretty serving bowl and lets it cool a bit.

6. While it is cooling, she washes and dries each strawberry with a paper towel. She puts the strawberries on a large plate with the bowl of chocolate sauce. She picks up each strawberry by the stalk and dips it into the sauce, then pops it quickly into her mouth. Yummy!

Recipe Index

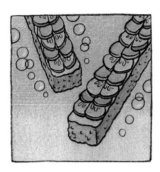